MONEY
MATTERS

Money Matters

21 PRACTICAL LESSONS FOR EVERYDAY SUCCESS

Adam Torres

Century City, CA

Edited by
Victoria Kirk
Michael Douglas Carlin

Century City, CA 90067
www.MrCenturyCity.com

The Mr. Century City Logo is a trademark of Mr. Century City, LLC.

ISBN: 0692794646
ISBN 13: 9780692794647
Library of Congress Control Number: 2016917815
Money Matters, Beverly Hills, CA

To all of my past, present and future mentors.

ACKNOWLEDGEMENTS

Writing a book is not an easy task. Special thanks to my editors Victoria Kirk and Michael Douglas Carlin for helping make this project a success. I appreciate all of your guidance and support on the revisions.

I would also like to thank the following individuals for their support throughout this effort.

Matt Cook, CEO of Mr. Century City, LLC.

Christopher Kai, KGL Consulting

Susan Bursk, President and CEO at Century City Chamber of Commerce

Barry LaValley, The Retirement Lifestyle Center

Yawei Cui Ph.D., Moody's Analytics

Jonathan Franklin, Law Offices of Jonathan Franklin

Katherine Koyanagi, Law Offices of Katherine Koyanagi

Dan Bienenfeld

Giancarlo Barraza, Founder of The Millionaire Mastermind

Claudio Juarez, Founder of Gotham City Crew

Matt Grey Ford, CEO of Urkli Marketing

CONTENTS

FOREWORD

I met Adam Torres before he created his Century City Wealth Management firm, when he was still working at a global financial advisory powerhouse. From the moment I met him at a keynote speech to now, I have consistently been impressed with his knowledge of how you can save, earn and invest your money.

We all know that "money matters" and Adam has done a great service by explaining to you in simple, straightforward terms how you can build a more sustainable financial foundation for you and your family.

Adam takes his commitments to clients, friends, family and community as serious as anyone I have ever met. This combined with his passion for helping others is why he is successful.

He is a mix between TV personality Jim Cramer, motivational guru Tony Robbins and sales expert Grant Cardone. He has the ability to teach while motivating and inspiring, all at the same time. Adam has the ability to take complex financial concepts and make them simple to understand.

In his book *Money Matters*, Adam walks you through the financial lessons he previously only shared with his thousands of clients, which include millionaires, successful entrepreneurs and executives. You are now holding the blueprint for your future financial success in your hand.

Read it. Devour it. Apply it. Begin living your dreams today.

Christopher Kai

INTRODUCTION

As I sit and think about how market challenges affect my clients, I can't help but need to make a difference. The market has been volatile, and all forecasts point to another rollercoaster of a year. I reflect on my meetings of the day, and the common themes of questions that pour in from clients: When will the Fed raise interest rates? What do you think about China? How can I earn more income from my investments? How do interest rates in Japan affect me? These are the questions that keep me up at night.

I am a student of the market and its vast behaviors. From my vantage point, it is apparent that individual client outcomes are, at many times, obvious (both the good and the bad). Just like the markets run in cycles, client investment decisions also have cycles. Some of these cycles are predictable—for instance, many clients have different investment objectives in retirement compared to when they were in the accumulation phase of their lives. However, some are not so apparent—like investors choosing to make the same mistakes time and time again.

Two glimmering examples of investors repeatedly making the same mistakes are the tech bubble burst in 2001-2002 and the mortgage meltdown in 2008. I very rarely find an investor who timed both crashes, and were able to effectively move from equities to cash. I am not claiming to have predicted either of these crashes—in fact, I did *not* see them coming. Frankly, market timing in the traditional sense is not a staple in my everyday business. My mission is to assess the appropriate risk reward scenario tailored to my clients' needs. The questions to ask yourself are: What have I learned from the recent crashes? Are my conclusions relevant and will they be useful in the future? Will I be prepared for the next crash?

Should you care about what I have to say? In an effort to persuade you to listen to my words, and give them some thought, I will give you my sales "pitch." In making this pitch thousands of times throughout the years, I have earned millions of dollars in assets under management (AUM). My words will resonate with some of you, and with others they will not. For those of you unaccustomed to what a "pitch" is, it is a rehearsed dialogue that should be delivered in a smooth, natural manner to explain your background and establish credibility. Here goes:

"My career in financial services began when I was 16 years old. I worked for Raymond James & Associates as an intern in their IRA department. I attended high school for roughly three hours a day before reporting to the firm. You could say I was groomed from a young age. I did not play sports in high school or college, because the market was and still is my passion and sport. After college, I worked for Vanguard for about 5 years before moving on to Charles Schwab, where I worked for another 5 years. I then decided to take the expertise I garnered at various firms to start my own firm, where I now customize plans to the needs of families I serve. At this point in my career, I have worked with over 2,000 clients and reviewed no less than 10,000 portfolios. I have found that each client is different, with different wants and needs. What are you looking to accomplish?"

The last sentence of my pitch is the most important: "What are you looking to accomplish?" The purpose of this book is to expand your understanding of investing concepts. Not the mundane parts of portfolio management, but the practical advice that everyone can use but rarely receive. Investment books can often be dry and boring. I chose to present this information in a format of stories and lessons. I find that learning through stories is more engaging and creates a better experience. I have also found that it can be more cost effective and efficient to learn from the experiences of others.

If this book helps you avoid just one of these discussed pitfalls, I have done my job and achieved my goal. In sharing these experiences and compiling my education for you, I hope to offer you new insights and ideas that you can apply directly to your finances. This is not a theory book. This is an action book of practical advice that is meant to be implemented today.

Too often I see investors not learning from mistakes of the past, and this is understandable. As someone once said: "It's hard to see the picture when you are standing in the frame." My goal is to guide you outside of your current frame of mind, and provide you with a different view that allows for better choices for your future.

To your success,

Adam

P.S. Check out my webpage www.AskAdamTorres.com for more tools to help you on your journey.

PART 1

MONEY MANAGEMENT MATTERS

SIMPLIFY YOUR LIFE WITH A SCRIPT

Lesson: Financial plans are vital to successfully directing your life.

I magine a huge movie set: there are bright lights, flashing cameras and a hard-working production crew moving everything around you. You are the director of your own movie. All eyes are on you while you control the environment surrounding you. With many decisions to make in only a split second, each decision has an immediate impact on the plot. Actors are looking at you waiting for direction, so you yell "action" and the scene unfolds. It is time to make your next decision, but you look down at the script only to find a blank page.

I find that this is how most people run their financial lives. The stakes are high, and the ramifications of a decision have long-lasting impacts, yet many people are working without a script—or in industry terms, a Financial Plan. Think of it like this: a financial plan is the movie script to your life. While directing your life, you may find that you would like to change the script or plan—and that's okay, but without direction, you are basically left guessing.

When working with clients, it is always my goal to help them craft the script of their lives. Unfortunately, clients often do not see the value of this exercise. If they have never composed a plan in the past, they wonder why they should create one now—especially when it can be a long process depending on the client's financial situation. An organized script improves the quality of a film, much like developing a financial plan improves your quality of life and chance of making informed investment decisions.

Financial plans vary in complexity and length. When you are young, your plan might resemble a short film. The budget may be low, and the plot may be simple. For example, you probably aren't married with kids if you just graduated from college. In fact, you may just be getting your first real job. The last thing on your mind is retirement, and I understand that. However, you will put yourself on the right path early in your career if you start the habit of planning now. This can potentially change your financial, professional and personal life as you move forward.

As you move through life, you are likely to add complexity to your script. The length of your movie is now longer, resembling a good documentary. You now have different sets, shots and scenes. There are far more people involved with the production, and the same rings true with your financial plan. You may be married with children. You've moved up the ladder in your career, and your earnings have probably grown. The assets you're investing have grown as well, and now you are considering branching out to other types of investments. If you are at this point in your life, and you have not created a financial plan, it isn't too late. Do it now! It will make a difference, especially in enhancing your retirement.

As you near retirement, your assets have hopefully grown. Your script may look more like a big-budget blockbuster movie, with occasional plot twists and turns. You have accumulated wealth and your situation may be complex. Your stage in life may overshadow the money you have accumulated, and every stage in life is an opportunity to reevaluate and incorporate changes. Never assume that you are on the right path financially, or that everything will be always be okay, because life throws unexpected plot twists often. Adjustments to the plan and follow-through can provide us with peace of mind by knowing you are on a productive path.

Most of the clients I work with are typically in the most productive stage of their lives or further along. I assist many of these clients in creating their first financial plan, probably because most people tend to get more serious about finances as they near retirement. If you are in this stage of your life, creating a plan should be on the top of your "to do" list. Don't leave your future to chance.

So what is involved in a financial plan? Some of the simple components can include the following:

Long Term & Short Term Goals:
Your goals should be specific, measurable and realistically relative to your situation.

Tax Planning:
Review tax returns to maximize tax savings, and ensure your tax planning matches the rest of your situation.

Investment Planning:
Review investments to determine if the portfolio is consistent with your overall objectives.

<u>Estate Planning</u>
Review estate documents, such as wills and trusts.

<u>Insurance Planning</u>
Analyze current policies and insurance coverage.

<u>Education Planning</u>
Discuss education goals and a plan to attain them.

<u>Implementation:</u>
The most important element is putting your plan into action, because all the planning in the world is meaningless unless it yields results.

Instead of breaking down the long list of planning components, we have covered just the most important basics of financial planning. The goal is simple: start writing your financial script. Your situation is unique from someone else's, and your plan will reflect your individual needs and goals. You should also have a few other components depending on your situation, such as a Balance Sheet, a Cash Flow Statement or a variety of other elements.

So what is the point of creating this plan?

Creating a financial plan is about empowerment, helping you feel secure and knowing you are working towards achieving your goals and future. I have guided clients to complete financial transformations—not because they had some windfall that made them wealthy, but because for the first time in their lives, they had a grasp on their financial situation. They finally understood how their day to day decisions affected their entire financial picture. Confidence in financial decisions can and will give you a renewed outlook on life.

These are some of the basic questions that could be answered after creating a financial plan:

1) Am I saving enough to reach my retirement goal or goals in general?
2) What rate of return do I need to achieve on investments to maintain my quality of living in retirement?
3) What amount can I spend in retirement so my money does not run out?
4) When can I retire?

The above questions may not be the "hot buttons" that motivate you to take action on creating your plan. For some of you, they may be exactly what you need to hear. Either way, the point here is that you can and should get started immediately. The sooner you go down the path of planning, the better. You can find many online calculators and sites to aid you, or you can seek the help of a professional advisor.

If you write your personal script, you will not be staring at a blank page the next time you have an important financial decision to make. You will also have the luxury and peace of mind to refer to your very own financial plan. Your confidence in tackling decisions will skyrocket because you will be able to ask yourself this simple question: "Is this decision going to bring me closer to my goals, or take me further from them?" Knowing the answer to that question alone can make all the difference.

The movie of your life is running and you are in the director's chair. Do you have a script in order, or are you just guessing what will happen next?

Things to remember:

1) A financial plan is like the movie script of your life.
2) It is never too soon or too late to begin planning.
3) Financial plans aide you in important decision-making throughout your entire life.

LIFE PRESERVERS SAVE LIVES

Lesson: Keep an emergency fund for unexpected expenses.

Emergencies always happen at the worst possible time, and they happen to all of us at some point in our lives. Everything will be seemingly fine; bills are paid and you feel like you are really making headway in your financial picture. Then suddenly—without warning—a storm hits. You lose your job, your car breaks down, you come down with an illness and cannot work, or some other unexpected dilemma places a financial obstacle in your path. Weathering the storm may depend on smart planning and savings. When proper planning is absent, the feeling of drowning may result.

It isn't if dilemmas will come; it is a matter of when. I want you to get ahead of inevitable financial storms by building an emergency fund—an account set aside for the purpose of dealing with emergencies. The idea is that if something major occurs, you will be able to use earmarked assets to shoulder the burden, instead of relying on high interest debt options like credit cards.

Not having an emergency fund is financial suicide because you do not know when emergencies will take place. Think of your emergency fund as a life preserver. You may never have to use it. Ideally you would never have to even reach for it. But if you were to need it, it may mean the difference between life and death—or in this case, your financial freedom and peace of mind, or a potential life of financial misery.

Draining investments to cover emergency expenses can be avoided by building an emergency fund. Most of your investments will fluctuate, meaning that if an emergency occurs when an investment troughs, you will have to liquidate at an inopportune time and compound the pain. People also often tap into their 401(k)s to cover emergencies, but treating your 401(k)s like a loan can sabotage your likelihood of a comfortable retirement.

So just how much should you save in this emergency fund? The savings will vary. Depending on who you talk to, you will get a wide range of answers and standards. In order to assess how much is enough, you will want to look at your personal situation and possibly get professional advice.

Here are some general guidelines:

If you are self-employed and your income varies, you may consider having at least one year of expenses set aside in an Emergency Fund. One year is important to cover prolonged periods of reduced income or outright business reversal that requires substantial reinvestment. It is important to have that extra cushion since you sign your own check. When business owners do not create large emergency funds, they are forced to take out loans to stay afloat during financial dilemmas. Compound interest may build a portfolio, but when debt accumulates and paying out interest diminishes profit margins, it may take years to rebuild your business.

If you are not self-employed and your employment is pretty steady, you can consider decreasing the amount of your Emergency Fund to six months or less. This is a personal choice. If you are the only income earner in the household, and you have children, you may choose to have more than 6 months in your fund. If you are in a household with two incomes and no children, three months may even be adequate. Some of my clients in this situation have three months or less in emergency funds because their employment is extremely steady and predictable.

Building an emergency fund doesn't have to be complicated. Answer these three questions to get started:

1) How much are my monthly expenses?
2) How many month's reserves should I set aside?
3) How much money per month can I realistically contribute to build my Emergency Fund?

Once you have completed the steps outlined above, you must follow through. It is a waste of your time to create the plan and fail to execute. Even if it seems daunting after creating the plan, putting your plan into practice will yield tangible benefits. For some of you, building your emergency fund may take multiple years. However, building this fund avoids the need to incur credit card debt or forgo the loss of investment income that is reserved for much later in life. Your Emergency Fund will sustain you through a tough time.

Now that you have an idea of how much your emergency fund should be, and how much a month you are able to contribute, where should you keep it? Typically, the Emergency Fund should ideally be invested to minimize risk and preserve liquidity. Consider bank accounts and money market funds. In today's climate of low interest rates, that may not sound attractive because you will be getting a low rate of return on your money. But remember, the emergency fund needs to be extremely liquid and stable. The point of this fund is not to earn a large return, but to limit risk and be readily available to cover emergencies.

One trap that you do not want to fall into while building your emergency fund is forgoing investing altogether. It may take you years to build a solid fund, but this is more of a balancing act than an all-or-nothing proposition. It is important to practice sound financial habits, such as contributing to your company's 401k and amassing other investments. This is not a perfect science; it is more of an art, simply because you cannot predict when your next emergency will arise. You will have to weigh what works best for you.

An Emergency Fund is one of the most important staples to your financial wellness picture. Either calculate what you need yourself, or seek out the advice of a professional. Just remember that with financial storms on the horizon, your Emergency Fund can help you avoid drowning and provide you with peace of mind.

Things to remember:

1) Emergency funds vary based on employment and family status.
2) Self-employed individuals may need larger Emergency Funds to weather economic downturns.
3) Do not neglect basic investing, even if your Emergency Fund is not fully funded.

Forget Your Paycheck?

Lesson: Set aside a percentage of every paycheck for savings and investing.

Many households in the United States live paycheck to paycheck, and tend to follow a routine pattern after receiving one. After first paying their bills, they consider purchasing luxury items and other nonessentials. Finally, after the paycheck is nearly used up, they divvy up what should actually go into savings. Many people also use credit cards to supplement their spending habits, which can make the situation even worse. Unfortunately, this is a disastrous cycle that has led to extremely low savings rates and underfunded retirements in the United States—but, this cycle can be broken based off of one simple concept: Pay Yourself First.

Clients often ask for advice on accumulating savings, and when I tell them to pay themselves first, they are usually shocked. They are instead looking for a magical formula that will make everything work in their financial lives. Through the years, I have witnessed many clients increase their net worth each year paying themselves first, combined with sound money management. To grow your net worth, change the model you use to handle money. Review the two models below, and adopt the new one.

Old Model:

1) Make retirement plan contribution (if you are not doing this, start immediately).
2) Pay bills.
3) Cover nonessentials and luxury items, vacations etc.
4) PAY YOURSELF!

New Model:

1) Make your retirement plan contribution.
2) PAY YOURSELF a percentage of your income.
3) Pay bills.
4) Cover non-essentials and luxury items, vacations etc.

The new model works. Some of you might doubt your ability to follow the plan, because you're barely capable of paying your bills. The key here is to just start. The starting percentage you pay yourself does not have to be high, especially if this is a new concept to you. The ultimate goal should be paying yourself at least 10% of your income before paying bills or purchasing non-essential items. My friend's son is lucky to be buying a home after implementing this exact practice. When the boy started working at age 16, he developed the discipline of saving 10% of his income. Now, in his early 20s, he is purchasing a home. It may takes years to successfully reach your goal, but the accomplishment is rewarding.

Don't get hung up on the 10% number. For some of you, that may be too much. For others, that may not be enough. While I do know that debts and obligations from emergencies will rear their ugly heads and get in the way, this is exactly why you should prioritize paying yourself first. It is never convenient to save. Something always comes up. Hasn't it been that way in the past? And it is likely that it will be that way in the future—unless you choose to change. People constantly play defense with their money and pay bills as they come in. By paying yourself first, you begin playing offense and give yourself a chance to score a successful financial future.

Another benefit to paying yourself will be your sense of financial accomplishment and freedom. It is extremely discouraging to look at your paycheck at the end of the month and not know where it all went. Working hard without the feeling of progress in life is the worst feeling—and the longer this goes on, the more discouraging your financial life can get. This will affect performance at work and family life. You will feel much better seeing your assets accumulate, while your debt decreases. Small amounts saved over time become large meaningful amounts.

For this plan to work, it must become a habit. Inconsistency will severely limit your likelihood of this plan being successful. Just like going to the gym, going once or twice will not produce results. You must go consistently to see true change. If possible, make paying yourself automatic. I advise clients to meet with their employer to first set up paying themselves. Many employers allow direct deposits to more than one bank account. I have clients direct a percentage of their income into a bank account that they do not even look at. Many times this account is set up at a bank that they do not normally use. I also encourage them to not monitor the account often—they should simply act like the money is no longer theirs while it continues to add up.

Bills and other obligations are a fact of life and part of being an adult, but at some point, you must take control of your financial life. You don't want to look back at a lifetime of work and continuously feel like you have no idea where your paycheck went. You have to pay the most important person in the equation–yourself.

Things to remember:

1) Debt and other obligations always creep up on you.
2) You will feel better about your financial situation once your assets and net worth begin increasing.
3) Engrain the habit of paying yourself first, and you will be on the path to financial freedom.

HOUSING BALL AND CHAIN

Lesson: Assess personal goals when considering renting versus buying a home.

When I first arrived in Phoenix, Arizona in 2006, the housing market was extremely hot by any measure. Homes were selling for record prices and a refinance boom was taking place. People were literally using their homes as cash registers, taking equity out of them up to three times a year. Many home owners participating in this behavior counted on home values to continue rising. If values plateaued or plummeted, homeowners would be over-leveraged and unable to maintain their lifestyle because they could no longer refinance their homes. The housing crisis of 2008 brought this behavior to a screeching halt. Many lessons were learned, but the memories are short.

They forgot a simple concept: housing prices do not always rise. Housing prices were rising for such a long time that people forgot home prices could actually level out, or even fall. This simple piece of advice is how I begin conversations with clients about renting or buying a home. When asking yourself whether you should rent or buy a home, I urge you to consider the following question: *What if you purchase a home and the value decreases?*

A decrease in home value does not affect most people immediately, because they bought their homes to live in long-term. If you plan on only being in a city for a couple of years, it might not make sense to purchase a home. Using the 2008 crash as an example, if you had purchased a home in Phoenix in 2006, and were planning on moving to another city in 2009, it is highly unlikely that you would have been able to sell your home. Many homeowners in the Phoenix market found themselves in this situation.

In assessing your personal situation, cash flow should be a major factor. You never want to find yourself in a position where you are "housing poor." This is where an inordinately large percentage of your income goes to covering housing. Depending on where you live, it may make sense to own versus renting because buying a home is cheaper than renting in some markets. In other markets, renting is cheaper than buying a home. In evaluating this decision, make sure to work with a professional realtor and financial advisor to estimate unforeseen costs. I have seen unexpected costs completely change the financial outlook of a home purchase versus renting. You need to know the unforeseen costs, such as a timetable for a roof replacement. If you are renting a home and the roof needs to be replaced, it is the landlord's problem. If you own the home, it becomes your problem. The last thing you want to do is become a slave to your home's unexpected expenses. I have seen many people work just to maintain their homes, and it is not a pretty situation.

The next thing to consider is the down payment. I am frequently asked if it makes sense to make a higher down payment, or stick with the minimum. Of course, my answer varies from situation to situation, but I will give you some general guidelines. When you put more money down on your loan, you will have a lower monthly payment because less of the home's purchase will be financed. You're borrowing less from the bank, which also means you will pay less interest over time. Some people prefer this because they feel safer having borrowed less and prefer to see a smaller bill. Some clients say less debt allows them to sleep better at night, but this does not always make investment sense. The down payment money will now be locked into the home value as potential equity, because it is not always easy to take money out of the home if you need it in the future.

On the other hand, some clients prefer to make the lowest down payment possible. Of course, this typically means a higher payment because you borrow more from the bank. You will also be paying more in interest over the course of the loan. However, this option gives you the benefit to divert money to other uses. These uses could include investing in something else for the potential of a higher return. It could also beef up your savings, or pay down other debt if applicable. The point here is that you will have more flexibility with your money if you choose a lower down payment. Realistically, there is no right or wrong answer to the down payment question. You really need to assess your own goals and risk tolerance to decide if more or less works best for your situation.

Let's say that you've assessed your goals and are leaning towards purchasing. The final question to ask yourself: Is it the right time to buy? Depending on the market, purchasing a home may not currently be an attractive value. The housing market runs in cycles, so you ultimately need to decide where in the cycle you want to buy. Don't feel like you have to rush into a purchase immediately. I waited four years before making a purchase in Phoenix because I couldn't justify the inflated prices. If you plan on being in your home long-term, it makes sense to wait for the right opportunity. Remember, for many, this will be one of the largest purchases of their lives.

The lessons of 2008 have already been forgotten by many. While some consider a home a long-term commitment, others consider it a speculation tool. Both speculation and the long-term buy and hold of a property can work. Just consider that home values do not always rise. Only purchase a home if it matches your individual situation and goals. Otherwise, renting may be the better option.

Things to remember:

1) Home values do not always go up.
2) Assess your long-term goals before renting or buying a home.
3) Assess the housing market before making a purchase.

Navigate The Mortgage Maze

Lesson: Choose a mortgage option that meets your specific goals.

My first real job out of college was for a large mortgage company, and I still recall how daunting it was to look at a matrix of mortgage products that I not only had to know, but also had to explain and sell. Looking back at that experience, I understand how people can get lost when shopping for a mortgage. It seems like every time you turn around, a new mortgage product is offered and you want to make the right decision. The correct decision determines the difference between long term success and failure when financing your home.

Whether you are in the market to purchase a new home or refinance an existing loan, it makes sense to match financing options with your goals. I find that people are often focused solely on the interest rate, and while this is a good start, it doesn't take into account the entire picture. I will outline other considerations when deciding which financing options fit your situation best.

When making a home purchase, it is essential to examine cash flow and the percentage of income that will be spent on the new home. If you are currently renting, you may consider how much your payment will be, including expenses like taxes and maintenance. Once you have a good ballpark number, you should ask yourself whether you are buying too much home, or if you can afford more. Just because a bank is willing to loan you money does not mean you should take it. I have seen clients purchase a much bigger home than intended because they were approved for a larger amount. This could be financial suicide if you take on too much, and then experience a financial emergency. You want to ensure that the mortgage option you choose allows you to make comfortable payments in both good times and bad.

The lowest payment is not always the best option. Consider whether or not your goal is to pay down some of the principal in the home throughout the term of your loan. An interest-only option mortgage may provide you with the lowest payment, but it requires discipline in adding additional principal if you ever want to pay the mortgage down. If you choose not to pay down your mortgage, you will have to refinance the mortgage eventually, which simply means paying off the current mortgage with another loan. Most interest-only loan options have a date that the rate and payment may adjust. If we are in a financial disaster, such as the housing crisis of 2008, refinancing may not be an option. So what happens in this scenario? Many people had loan adjustments they were unable to refinance. Combine this with potential drastic payment increases that many were not able to pay, and the result was that many lost their homes. Do you have the discipline to add that extra payment? If not, and your goal is to pay down the loan to build equity, it makes sense to consider another option.

Refinancing is a popular option for many existing homeowners. The reasons you would refinance typically include consolidating debt, taking equity out of your home or lowering your interest rate over the term of the loan.

Refinancing solely for the sake of lowering your interest rate doesn't always make sense. You really want to ask yourself how long you plan on being in your home. Many homeowners refinance to get a lower rate, even though they did not plan on keeping their home. Take into consideration how much it will cost you to refinance a mortgage, because the fees could outweigh the benefits depending on how long it will take you to break even. For example, if it takes you 5 years to break even on the cost of refinancing, it probably doesn't make sense to refinance if you are thinking of relocating or selling your home soon. The fees will then outweigh the benefit of the reduced interest rate, unless you stay in the home for at least five years.

Refinancing to consolidate debt can be a great option when the numbers make sense. The numbers make sense when you lower the overall interest you pay on the debt and take refinancing costs into account. It is usually best to take any savings from the lower payment and apply it to paying down other outstanding debt. People get themselves in trouble when they refinance, consolidate debt and potentially lower their interest rate. These are all good things, but when they take this new found financial position as a green light to spend more, they are ultimately taking on even more debt. Using a credit card's zero balance as an invite to take a vacation isn't a necessity or immediate need. Instead, use your new found financial position to add to your assets or pay off other debt.

Pulling equity out of your home is something to carefully consider. Some look at equity in the home as money that could be used for upgrades or other items. Others look at their home's equity as a nest egg for retirement. Your chosen view is your personal preference, and whether or not it makes sense financially varies per situation. It also depends on the amount of equity you have accumulated, and what the potential uses of it would be. Consult your financial advisor to see what makes the most sense for your situation.

In today's low interest rate climate, the duration of a mortgage is not discussed as often as it has been in the past—but it should still be evaluated carefully. The most common types of loans are 30-year, 15-year, 7-year ARMs (adjustable rate mortgage), and 5-year ARMs.

When examining your goals, determine whether or not it makes sense to choose a 30-year mortgage. A 30-year mortgage usually comes with higher interest rates and cost more. Homeowners enter 30-year mortgages for the feeling of safety, because the interest rate will not adjust like it would with an ARM. But, most people do not pay off their homes. Most homeowners either refinance their mortgage, or sell the home long before the payoff date. Very few people actually live in their homes for 30 years, so paying extra interest may not make sense.

I understand that the mortgage maze can be confusing. The first matrix I had to decipher made my head spin. Financing options are not getting any less complicated, and they are likely to continue evolving. Managing one of the largest debts you may ever owe deserves careful planning, so take your time and choose wisely.

Things to remember:

1) Take into account your cash flow when choosing a mortgage.
2) Depending on your goals, refinancing to consolidate debt, lower your interest rate and pull equity out of your home can be good options.
3) The duration of your mortgage should coincide with your goals.

THE DIRT ON DEBT

Lesson: Some forms of debt are beneficial while others can be tragic.

D ebt is a dirty word to many people. In most households, it's almost a taboo subject. Nobody wants to face the reality of large credit card bills, mortgages, car loans or other forms of debt. Some are even afraid to open the mail because of what might be lurking. Contrary to popular belief, debt should not be treated as the elephant in the room. Instead, debt should be used as a tool to achieve your goals. Now, this doesn't mean you should go out and max out credit cards. First, you must educate yourself on debt and its proper uses.

Many people use a mortgage to purchase a home. This is viewed by many as a great way to grow your asset base while investing a minimal amount. For example, if you put down a down payment on a home and finance the rest, you control an asset for a fraction of the home's value. This is an important concept to understand because if the total value of the home appreciates, you benefit from the appreciation. Alternatively, if the home depreciates, you are on the hook if you choose to sell the devalued property. A mortgage is one way to use debt in a responsible manner, as long as the home is within your price range and matches your long-term goals.

If you are a real estate investor, you may take the above concept and expand your debt and asset base by taking on more than one property. While this may be more complicated, and will take more attention than just owning your primary residence, it is an option that many should explore. Real estate can be a great option for someone who doesn't mind doing the work, has a solid balance sheet and has mentorship from an experienced investor. If you choose this route, it is likely you will have multiple mortgages. When executed properly over time, this is not a bad thing.

Other examples of responsible debt include student loans for furthering education. I know this is a controversial subject— many do not believe that an education is what it used to be. Many believe that the current high cost of education has outpaced incomes for certain professions. For example, if you are pursuing a career as an elementary school teacher and need to finance your education, the prospect of paying back the loans quickly is unrealistic. Even some traditionally higher paying professions— like lawyers—also find themselves with debt burdens. I am not here to pass judgment on whether or not it's a good idea for you or your children to go to school. However, an education can never be taken from you, regardless of if you go to school or are self-taught. Seek education in some form if you want to remain competitive in the constantly evolving workforce.

Revolving debt lands people in rough waters. Relying on credit card debt to continue a lifestyle you cannot afford is not sustainable. I have seen people put $4,000 and $5,000 vacations on credit cards because they didn't have the money in the bank. This type of behavior will destroy your financial future. If you are still paying off a vacation that took place two years ago, something is wrong. At some point, you have to be realistic with yourself and delay the gratification of getting something now with a credit card, and save for the future instead. If this habit of saving for the future is not adopted, you may be leaving your future to chance.

Another item that is usually funded through debt is a car. If you must take out a loan to purchase a car, there is nothing wrong with that. You do have to get to work one way or another. I advise keeping your car purchase in line with what you can actually afford. When completing financial plans for clients, I have actually seen automobile payments larger than their mortgage. This would be fine if they weren't severely underfunding their retirement, and had little to no Emergency Fund or savings. Driving an automobile that may not be the newest model is a simple choice that can put you further ahead in life. The second you drive a car off the lot, it depreciates significantly. Consider putting the extra money into assets that can actually increase in value instead.

If you struggle with debt and are currently underwater, don't worry—you are in good company. Many are in the exact same situation. The key to breaking the cycle is developing positive habits. Here are steps you can follow to break bad debt habits:

1) Do not add more consumer debt, like credit cards.
2) Set a goal to pay off your current consumer debt.
3) Every time you consider adding debt, ask yourself the following questions:
   A) Is this good debt or bad debt?
   B) Does adding this debt bring me closer to my goals, or further from them?
   C) If this is bad debt, can I live without this purchase?

It sounds simple, but this is really the first step. If you can consistently complete these three steps over time, your debt will decrease while your assets increase. Of course the plan should be tailored to your situation, so either do it yourself or seek the help of an experienced financial planner.

Getting your hands dirty while digging yourself out of bad debt may not be pleasant. Many will not have the stomach for the long and tedious process. After all, it's much more fun to get into debt then to get out of it. Right? Who wants to save for a vacation for two years, when you can charge it now and pay it off over the next four years? Right? Wrong! Stop paying interest to others and start investing in yourself. Don't treat debt as a dirty word. Instead, educate yourself about it and use it to your advantage. Make good debt your ally, and go to war with the bad.

Things to remember:

1) Debt can be your friend when you use it to grow assets.
2) Taking on debt for non-essential depreciating assets can sabotage you.
3) If you struggle with debt, create a plan to pay it off.

AUTOMATE YOUR SUCCESS

Lesson: Reach your goals by automating financial decisions.

E nforcing a routine habit is hard to do—especially when it requires a not-so-pleasant commitment. Most people wish to incorporate a gym habit into their lives, and work out several times a week. However, we all know that can be can be a hit-or-miss feat, depending on the week and person. For many of us, hitting the gym can be a series of false starts. I personally am pretty streaky— I can be on for a couple of years, and then off for an entire year. Sometimes I make progress, but then fall behind when I'm not dedicated to frequenting the gym. The same rings true for our finances—financial habits can be hard to accommodate.

Adopting financial health habits is just as important as fitness habits—if not more so. Money problems inevitably lead to high stress, which can certainly affect a person's overall health and wellbeing. Focusing on financial health in combination with fitness can dodge emotional stress, which has been previously linked to disease and sickness in the body.

How can we make programing beneficial financial habits less of burden? The solution is automating certain financial habits, which can lead to successfully reaching financial goals.

First, you should automate investing. If you have a 401(k), or company retirement plan at work, you are likely already contributing to it automatically. If not, maybe it's time to start. The idea is that you will not even notice the money being invested, and you cannot spend it because it never touched your hands. This is a really important concept. You do not have to display an exceptional amount of self-control and savings ability, because you take the decision out of your hands. The concept is much like someone trying to cut out certain foods from their diet—if they never walk into a McDonald's, it is very unlikely that they will ever eat there. If the money never touches your hands, it is more difficult to spend.

You also want to automate the yearly percentage increase of your 401(k) contributions. Most employers have an option to do this, which makes it relatively simple. Raise your contribution from your salary every year by at least 1-2%. Clients utilize this method to allot the maximum allowed amount to their 401(k) plans. Understand, they did not meet with me and decide to give up all enjoyable things in life to put money into their 401(k). Instead, they used the process to gradually "max out" their 401(k) contributions throughout the years, without even noticing it in many cases. This is a great way to really boost your retirement savings.

Let's say you already reached the contribution limit of your 401(k), and have money left over—or maybe you just do not want to tie up money in a company retirement plan because you are looking for a shorter-term investment. You may want to consider opening a brokerage account. Think of a brokerage account as an account that holds investments, but are now potentially taxable. Most brokerage accounts allow you to purchase mutual funds, and also set those up for automatic investment. Ideally, your company will allow you to direct deposit into multiple accounts. If this is the case, simply designate what percentage of your income you would like to contribute to your various accounts.

Now it is time to consider automating your savings to build up an Emergency Fund. You should have a separate untouchable account, used only in extreme times. As I mentioned earlier in this book, assess how much you need to save and start contributing to that goal—whether it is 3 months, or one year of expenses.

Some choose to go the entrepreneurial route. If you have a goal of starting a business, or want to make another type of investment, you might consider setting up a separate bank account. Label the account as an exploratory account, and set up a certain percentage per paycheck to contribute to this mission. I have instructed many clients with the dream of owning their own business to start saving for it. I am not against raising capital and borrowing to start a business, but while someone is working toward a dream, setting aside money to fund it is imperative. It allows time to think more clearly, and truly evaluate if the path you are going down is good for you.

Now that we have discussed automating the assets of your balance sheet, let's talk about liability. People are more likely to use automatic bill pay than automatically invest in something other than their employer's retirement plan. This is dangerous because at times, we commit to financial obligations we do not always remember. I once paid a gym membership fee for over a year to a gym I did not even attend. I moved to another area, and completely forgot to cancel the old membership because it was paid automatically. I know I am not the only who has ever done this.

Automating bill pay while not investing or saving is backwards. Consider this: Why should I be rushed to see money leave my bank account, instead of investing money into an asset? Don't get me wrong, I understand automatic bill pay—I use it too. But I also use automatic investing to my advantage. Utilizing one without the other is detrimental. Try incorporating both tools to achieve greater financial success.

Remember that the easiest way to ingrain a financial habit is to stay consistent—automate that habit! Automatic investing can be your best friend, while automatic bill pay could separate you from true expenses, and whether or not you need to cut them down. Automate your finances and get off the financial treadmill.

Things to remember:

1) Automate investing.
2) Automate saving.
3) Selectively automate bill payments.

PART 2

INVESTING FOR SUCCESS

DON'T DIE AT YOUR DESK

Lesson: Take advantage of your company's retirement plan.

You might want to be the next Mark Zuckerberg and establish the next social media platform that will change the world—or maybe you favor Elon Musk, and want to change the course of an entire industry. Your reward for completing either of these could be a billionaire fortune. You are working on your dreams and might be laser focused, and I am a huge fan of ambition and focus on achieving goals. But, sometimes that focus can blind you from the obvious. Contributing to your company's retirement plan is an obvious resource that many overlook. Don't give up on your dreams—but if you are not the next Internet billionaire, you may regret not deferring a portion of your salary to your company's retirement plan.

When I meet with a client for the first time, I always inquire about their company's retirement plan and if they participate. Many companies offer retirement plans, yet employees often opt out of this benefit. In fact, many employers now automatically enroll employees into retirement plans. If an employee chooses to opt out, they are typically required to sign a form because the company does not want liability down the line for an employee's poor choice. Think about that for a moment: Would you sign away your health care if you were not covered elsewhere? Probably not. So why sign away retirement benefits?

Most people do not participate in their 401(k)s because they do not understand the significance of participating. A common objection I hear from recent college graduates is that they cannot afford to make contributions, and will contribute when they hold a higher paying job. Unfortunately, this can be a huge mistake. Small contributions early in life are essential for long-term success. Lack of money is only one excuse I hear for not participating, but if you are interested in long-term success, I would argue that you cannot afford to not participate.

Most people do not understand that they are responsible for the majority of their retirement income. Even if social security is available when you retire, it is not meant to meet all of your needs. It is only intended to supplement living standards. Decisions you make now affect your quality of life down the line, and family dynamics related to retirement have evolved in the United States. This must be acknowledged to prepare for the future and what it is likely to bring.

In the past, grandparents and great-grandparents have had pensions. Think of a pension as a paycheck for the rest of your life. The company you dedicated 20-30 years of your life typically supported this paycheck, and was more of a paternalistic model. The company essentially served a parent type role, and gave you an allowance when you retired to reward you for many years of hard work. This money, combined with Social Security, could allow you to live out the rest of your days comfortably. Unfortunately, two major trends took place that no longer make this type of retirement planning possible.

In today's climate, it is very unlikely you will work for any company for 20 plus years. Think about it: can you honestly say that you will retire from your current company? Even those who own companies are not necessarily wanting to run it for 30 years, and may prefer to be bought out at some point. When I worked for someone else, the average time I spent with a company was 4-5 years. This is common for my social network, and many others. Even those who have worked for a company for 10 or more years would often times move on for the right opportunity. Compared to what it once was, company loyalty is rare in today's workplace.

Employers transitioned from offering pensions to the 401(k) system in the 70s. This is out of your control, but supports taking responsibility for your own retirement. The 401(k) was beneficial to companies because it released them from the burden of caring for retired employees for the rest of their lives. The added benefit was that the plan was portable, and could move with an employee from company to company. Funds could also be transferred to your own Individual Retirement Account (IRA) after severance from an employer. Companies are not required to guarantee retirement plans, and you are responsible for underlying investment choices. This frees up the company from acting as a parent, and allows them to focus on running their business.

I urge clients to sign up for their company's retirement plan. You control the amount automatically invested each paycheck. Think about it this way: you are paying yourself automatically before anyone else gets a piece of your check. You don't have to think about it because it's done automatically. As a general rule, I suggest increasing the percentage contributed every year by at least 1-2 percent. If you have been procrastinating, stop now! Take responsibility and move forward with your future. A much more aggressive deferral schedule will be more beneficial for some, but do something.

If you are a recent college graduate with dreams to create the next Facebook, I hope this convinced you to still participate in your current company's retirement plan. I want you to make that first billion, but if it doesn't happen, it's important that you survive and find comfort in retirement. If you are further along in your career, and still aren't participating in your company's retirement plan, consider this a wakeup call. You are responsible for your own retirement—the sooner you start investing, the better your odds for achieving retirement goals.

Things to remember:

1) You are responsible for your own retirement income.
2) Pensions are no longer an option for most people.
3) Automatic investing into your 401(k) is a great way to pay yourself before anyone else.

INVESTING ISN'T GAMBLING

Lesson: Diversification is crucial for most investors.

I f we all would have implemented Lieutenant Dan's investing from the famous Tom Hanks movie, "Forrest Gump," we
would have all bought Apple when it was trading at a mere
fraction of today's price. If you don't recall the movie, Lieutenant
Dan invested in Apple when it was a startup. Holding that one
stock over time would have made you quite wealthy. These are
the types of stories that lure investors into trying to "pick a winner." There are many dangers inherent in that approach—for
every Apple, there are thousands of companies that bust. Who
wants to base their investment future on picking the right company's stock? Or even the correct couple of stocks? Is this a realistic scenario for success? No!

Attempting to pick one stock that performed like Apple is
not realistic for most investors. For most of us, this approach is
more akin to gambling. Very few should take that approach—
just as very few should be professional poker players. For all of

the stock pickers reading this, or poker players for that matter, don't give up your dreams of picking a winner. By all means, I hope you pick the next Apple—but don't neglect traditional portfolio management techniques if you hope to increase the probability of your success. I recommend a diversified approach.

So what is diversification? It's a word that is often used, but rarely understood. It has even gained a subjective slant throughout the years. Once upon a time, diversifying a portfolio meant owning 20-30 stocks instead of one or two. Investors would purchase different stocks that represented different "sectors" or areas. Owning stocks in different sectors allows using various cycles of the market to your advantage, especially sectors that were doing well when others were not. This is an important concept to investing, but it is not the only variable involved in diversifying a portfolio.

Throughout the years, diversification has evolved from an infant state to the mature state it represents today. Now we focus not only on the sectors, but also on the asset classes and investment markets. Simply put, diversification means owning multiple markets in varying amounts. This means not only having exposure to the U.S. Markets, but also International Markets. These markets are ingredients, and for most investors, the recipe uses only one ingredient from each country. This ingredient was domestic stock. Now that the markets have changed with the tastes of investors, the recipe calls for many more "ingredients" from all around the world. These ingredients can be stocks, bonds, real estate and other investments.

So what is the point of creating a diversified portfolio? One goal is spreading the risk. Some portfolios have exposure to over 20 sectors and asset classes. Through the use of mutual funds, these portfolios can contain thousands of stocks and bonds. This strategy works because no advisor has the proverbial "crystal ball." Predicting the future of each individual investment is unrealistic. It is also not the advisor's role; he is not a psychic. What is realistic, however, is forecasting the performance in different markets, and gaining exposure to markets through various investments. In this manner, an advisor can analyze the past performance of markets to forecast a realistic rate of return and volatility. This doesn't guarantee results, but combined with other tools, this can be a solid approach.

There are arguments for and against diversification regarding performance. Some tested portfolios may concentrate investment in different areas, while attempting to also achieve a greater return than the overall market. Others argue that better performance can be achieved through concentrating investments into several sectors. If you solely consider performance when making investment decisions, consider long-term goals and not just the potential rate of return. Chasing rate of return has been the downfall of many investors. Some have ruined their investment lives when chasing the next hot investment. You cannot spend a rate of return—you spend money. Taking this into account, tailor your investment decisions based on goals and not on something as unreliable as rate of return.

Of course, there are other potential benefits of portfolio management concepts that are beyond this lesson. This is not intended to be a comprehensive review of diversification and other investment methods. Think of it like this: you spread the risk so that your future does not depend on the success of a few companies or markets. Nobody can predict the future of your investments at all times. You will be well on your way if you working within these constraints, combined with aligning investments and goals.

Don't get distracted. Focusing solely on picking winners can be a trap in the long run. Sometimes investors are successful while others are not. The idea of picking a winner is part of the reason casinos stay in business: the urge to gamble is too strong of one for most. Explore investment options, but don't forget the boring, old-fashioned diversification for the majority of your investing. If you are wrong about your stock, the boring portfolio will likely still be around if it is properly diversified.

Things to remember:

1) It is difficult to pick a winner.
2) Markets are more complex than they used to be.
3) Spreading the risk through diversification means owning more markets.

MAKING MONEY IN THE MARKET ISN'T A MIRACLE

Lesson: Savings rate can be more important than rate of return.

One question I receive more often than not is whether or not it is the "correct time" to enter the market. Investors ask this as if it is an all or nothing proposition. Some even make the potential mistake of being fully invested to cash, and back again. It's as if making money in the market depends on some cosmic event—the planets have to be aligned at just the right point, and investment timing needs to be done with a rocket's precision when taking off into outer space. Every system has to be running perfectly to bring the astronauts home, or in this case, everything has to be timed perfectly to have enough money for a comfortable retirement. I believe this scenario is far from the truth, and the market is much more forgiving for long-term, properly diversified investors.

Timing the market over an entire lifetime is an extremely difficult task. Some investors brag about getting out of the market before the tech wreck of 2002. However, many of these investors were then caught in the housing crisis of 2008—or maybe if we go further back, some were caught in the crash of 1987. The point here is that these crashes happen unexpectedly. Timing when they will happen and jumping out of the market prior to it happening is very unlikely. Let's say for a moment that you happen to call a crash and get out of the market prior—you may be feeling really good about your choice. Here is the problem though: when do you get back into the market? You called the top of the market, but are you also going to be able to call the bottom of the market? It rarely happens, especially over the course of many years. While some make it their life's mission to accomplish this feat, for the majority of us, this will not be the case. In accepting that it is unlikely for us to time the market consistently, what are we to do next?

I coach my clients to take the focus away from rate of return, and place the emphasis on savings rate. Think of your savings rate as the amount of money that you save versus your income. For example, if you save 5% of your income and put that in your 401(k), is that really enough? Depending on how much you earn, versus how much you spend, a 5% savings rate may be adequate. For some of you, a much higher savings rate may be preferable. You are in control of your savings rate, and it's something you can increase and decrease over time. You will not always be in control of your rate of return, or volatility in your portfolio, but savings rate can be altered at your discretion.

Your savings rate is something that will change over time. I like to compare savings rate to getting fitted for a suit. Your size or rate will certainly fluctuate, depending on your situation. If your income fluctuates sharply, you will have to increase and decrease your savings rate more often. Let's say you are self-employed and experience both good and bad years. During good years, you may want to save much more than you would in a lean year. Take advantage of those banner years to quickly build up your savings, because you do not know when the next big payday may come. If your income is relatively the same, your savings rate has a less volatile measurement or relationship to your goals. In this case, keep your rate relatively consistent and if it makes sense, increase the rate gradually over time.

I understand that it is extremely unlikely to hear people in the United States brag about their savings rate—we have some of the worst savings rates in the world. We are a trained consumer society, and many in the United States live paycheck to paycheck while neglecting savings altogether. Talking about rate of return is a much sexier topic for us. The concept of investing a little and making a lot of money is much more appealing to most, but it is not realistic. Instead focus on what you can control for a better result, and you'll find a stronger chance of reaching your goals.

Now that you are a little more educated on savings rates and rate of return, I hope you begin focusing on both—especially if you give savings rate no attention at all and focus merely on rate of return. Focus on your savings rate to avoid becoming "retirement poor" and inevitably feeling like your money is going to retirement with nothing left for fun. Instead, focus on savings rate as an empowering exercise that puts you in control. Successful retirement is not rocket science. It can actually be a pretty predictable journey when you understand it doesn't depend on wishing upon a shooting star.

Things to remember:

1) The reason to invest is not to beat the market—it is to reach your individual goals, such as maintaining your current lifestyle in retirement.
2) Focus on savings rate more than rate of return.
3) Your savings rate can fluctuate over time.

IS WARREN BUFFETT MISLEADING YOU?

Lesson: Buffett's style of investing may not work for you.

Warren Buffett may be the most famous investor of all time—I can visit offices as far away as China and see his picture displayed prominently. It's hard to not see him on TV giving commentary when something big happens in financial markets. I don't think anyone would argue against him being a brilliant man. Unfortunately, people go wrong with Buffett's brilliance when they attempt applying his ideologies to their own situations.

I don't think Buffett gives the general public bad investment advice—I am a big Buffett fan. I am not, however, a fan of the way people tend to digest his information. When he gets on TV and states that the bond market is not an attractive place to be at the moment, some investors take that as a sign to sell their bonds. Understand that when he does this, he is only giving general information. Many times, obvious and correct information— but this information is not tailored to your personal investment situation. If you are retiring soon, it is likely that you have bond exposure of some type, and use it for income and cutting down the volatility in your portfolio. Selling bonds because they are not producing the best return could be disastrous, depending on market conditions.

Buffett is "textbook" when it comes to his value investing approach, and he should be—he learned some of his views from Benjamin Graham, who is considered the "father" of value investing by many. I am not arguing against value investing versus another type of investing. Many investment philosophies help you reach your goals. Some subscribe to Modern Portfolio Theory, while some subscribe to others. Investors get themselves in trouble when they misinterpret investment philosophy.

To accumulate much of his wealth, Buffett has previously used a buy and hold strategy on investments for long periods of time. A handful of investments have made him and his early investors quite wealthy. Of course, I am over simplifying his ideology for the sake of brevity. Entire books are written on Buffett's investment style—Google it if you would like more detailed information. Investors misinterpret buy and hold strategies based off of a value approach for a "collection strategy." I advocate different "buy and hold" strategies combined with a rebalancing approach—what I do not advocate are collection strategies where investors collect stocks without regard for how they fit into a balanced portfolio. Some investors act like stocks are comic books. They have to hold onto them forever because some day, they may rise in value. I have seen investors hold portfolios of 50+ stocks, and not even remember the names of all stocks they had. It isn't pretty.

Buffett advocates that when buying stock, you should consider it in the literal sense. This is correct because you are purchasing the company—a very small portion usually, but still technically correct. The next thing you should do is have enough conviction in your investment to imagine the stock market closing down and not being able liquidate your shares. But how many people actually do enough research on a company before purchasing it to determine whether they should hold it for 10+ years? Not many. Most people cannot even name the CEOs of the companies they own. If you can name the CEO, can you name other officers in the company? If you can't name the leaders of the company, or any of the direct team members, how can you determine if they are leading their company in the right direction?

The last thing I propose you to consider on Buffett's investment path is that his positioning. You are not in his position. Buffett will most likely hold shares of Berkshire Hathaway for the rest of his life, without depending on any of it for living expenses. He will not liquidate a single share. He will also donate the bulk of his wealth. The majority of us, however, will not fall into this category. Most of us need some part of our assets to cover our lifestyle in retirement. This includes liquidating investments to support us. We may also have the goal of leaving some wealth to our children.

So what do I suggest you do?

Choose an investment style and portfolio that is customized to your goals. Include a financial plan and investment policy statement that you can buy into. For the majority of investors, products like mutual funds, exchange traded funds (ETFs) and Robo-Advisors make sense. Investing in individual stocks may not be very attractive for investors going forward. I see very few investors learning the fundamental approach that Buffett follows by picking up the 700-page "Security Analysis" tome by Benjamin Graham and David L. Dodd. Doing anything less than that means investing because off sound bites, and it can be a dangerous pursuit if the right one doesn't catch your attention at the right time.

Buffett's investment strategies made him one of the wealthiest men in the world. Trying to pattern your investment philosophy after his may seem like a good idea, and for many people it has worked out well. Make sure that if you do choose to go the Buffett route, you are properly educated and not misapplying his teachings.

Things to remember:

1) A buy and hold strategy is different from a collecting strategy. Accumulated stocks are not comic books.
2) Most people don't do enough research on a company to determine whether it is worth holding for 10+ years.
3) Invest based on a customized plan to meet your goals. If you are not super wealthy, you might need your assets to pay living expenses someday.

DON'T FEAR FRIENDLY ROBO-ADVISORS

Lesson: Robo-Advisors are perfect solutions for many investors.

When I hear people talk about robo-advisors, they talk about something out of a Terminator movie. They are most concerned that some form of artificial intelligence is replacing the human factor in our world. Picture Arnold Schwarzenegger as the Terminator, jumping out of your computer monitor and rebalancing your portfolio. As ridiculous as that sounds, many feel robo-advisors make traditional investment management extinct. Is this a plausible reality going forward, or an outlandish claim?

Let's define robo-advisor: A robo-advisor is a form of automated portfolio management. Algorithms are programmed to do the rebalancing or adjustments in the portfolio for you. This option is something most people "set and forget." All investment management is done seamlessly after setting it up, with little future maintenance because the algorithm manages it. Before robo-advisors were an option, the advisor or his support staff did this rebalancing manually. There are debates about whether or not the advisor added value by conducting this activity himself.

Robo-advisors can set up a well-balanced and diversified portfolio relatively quickly. Some online services can help you set up a portfolio in under 10 minutes—this means you will not have to spend much time choosing individual investments. You can simply answer the questionnaires and let the algorithm place you in the portfolio that best accommodates your risk tolerance and time horizon. These portfolios are typically model portfolios that the company has established. Some see this as a negative thing, but it can be positive. If a large company chooses to offer clients the option of choosing between 10 portfolios, those portfolios likely represent the company's best ideas on money management. It is highly unlikely that they will create a product they do not think is quality. They have too much to lose, considering the rise in attention given to robo-advisors. Just like it was simple to buy and sell stock online with the click of a button, you can now set up a portfolio with just a few clicks.

The potential drawback of robo-advisors is their tendency to be very inflexible. This may or may not be an actual drawback. In the past the traditional advisor may have held off on rebalancing a portfolio after a conversation with the client about their goals. This was seen as a "value add" and distinguished one advisor's performance from another's. Others feel that taking the human element out of the day to day ongoing investment decisions is a bonus because there is less room to deviate from the original investment objective. A Robo-Advisor simply does what it is programmed to do: Nothing less and nothing more. If the portfolio is out of balance, the robo-advisor algorithm will get it back in line. I have seen the human element hurt a portfolio, and situations where it has helped. Robo-advisors are a relatively new concept—more flaws and benefits will surely reveal themselves over time.

Ask yourself which option you feel suits you best. The reason I say "feel" is because this decision is a highly emotional one for many. Behavioral finance suggests that we often act based on emotion when making investment decisions. For some, depending on an algorithm to place you in the correct portfolio and maintain its balance seems scary, regardless if it earns a higher or lower return. Some prefer the human element, and I am completely fine with this. I do not think there is a right or wrong answer here, but I do not see much difference between the two approaches other than physically executing trades. When going through a series of questions with clients and assessing their goals, my brain functions much like an algorithm. It sends me in the correct direction for recommending a portfolio, and allows me to evaluate which changes I need to make. When implemented properly, there is nothing to fear in the robo-advisor approach.

For more complex existing portfolios, robo-advisors are not advanced enough to manage your assets yet, especially if your portfolio of individual stock cannot be liquidated without large tax implications. The best approach for this situation lies somewhere between a robo-advisor and a financial advisor. You still need a financial advisor to help with the financial planning process and investment management. For example, a robo-advisor cannot refer to many years of work with other clients to decipher whether or not you are making the correct financial decision. But a robo-advisor might make sense for your children that are new to investing.

Because investing will always be an emotional pursuit, a financial advisor's place in their clients' lives will remain intact. The relationship and trust developed over time between a client and advisor cannot be commoditized. As a client nears or enters retirement, the complexity of the situation cannot be put into a nice neat box. We are emotional beings that don't always make rational decisions—the likelihood of the financial industry being taken over by the Terminator or robo-advisors is highly unlikely. Human touch will always be needed in one form or another.

Things to remember:

1) Robo-advisors are an efficient way diversify a portfolio.
2) Robo-advisor portfolios are often built using the same principles that traditional advisors use.
3) Combining the investment management of a robo-advisor with the human touch of a traditional advisor is one balanced approach.

EXPERIENCE COMPOUND INTEREST

Lesson: Compound interest is an important investment ally. When you have debt, it is your worst enemy.

Compound interest—deemed a wonder of the world by many—is understood by few people. Its influence helps shape cultures and civilizations alike, and is the reason some cities have risen and fallen. The cities that harnessed its effect prospered greatly, and found their treasure chest overflowing with riches. Cities that fell victim to it were crushed by debt they could never escape. Many households today find themselves in this exact situation. When compound interest is on your side, it can make you a king of your domain. When it is not, you can become a servant to your possessions.

Compound interest is a simple concept to understand. It is the root of why many people have become wealthy over time. When investments are made, you may receive dividends, interest or some other form of payment. When you receive that return on your investment, simply investing it back into the same instrument puts compound interest to work. Let's say you own Apple stock. If Apple pays you a 2% dividend, and you decide to buy more Apple stock, you are reinvesting your dividends and compounding your investment. This gives you the opportunity to potentially grow your investments faster.

The following is a simple example of how $100 invested at a 7% interest rate compounded quarterly would look at different time intervals. This simply means that every year, 7% is paid on the amount invested over the course of 4 quarterly payments.

End of Year 1: $107.19
End of Year 5: $141.48
End of Year 10: $200.16
End of Year 20: $400.64
End of Year 30: $801.92

This might not seem like a big deal to you. You put away $100.00 and 30 years later, it has surpassed $800.00. This is not life changing money. Compound interest really becomes interesting when you make additional consistent investments over time. Let's take the same scenario from above and just start adding $100.00 to your investment each month. This may not be realistic for the outside investment world, because the interest or dividends may change over time on an investment, but it works for the "classroom" setting.

In the new scenario $100 is invested at a 7% interest rate compounded quarterly, with an additional $100 being added monthly.

End of Year 1: $1,353.40
End of Year 5: $7,334.76

End of Year 10: $17,570.33
End of Year 20: $52,538.91
End of Year 30: $122,531.91
End of Year 50: $543,049.11

As you can see, adding additional funds to your investment is crucial to amassing money over the long run. An extra $122,531.91 over 30 years—or $543,049.11 over 50 years—makes a difference. The example I used was based on investing an additional $100 a month. This is also not considering any potential appreciation of the investment. This is a really simple calculation, but if your investment actually rose in value, that may also inflate your return. Every employed individual should be able to invest $100 per month for retirement. Ideally, more would be better, but starting somewhere is key. The more time you have your money invested, the greater chance you have of amassing a respectable nest egg that allows you to live out your ideal retirement.

The longer you keep compounding the investment return, the greater the potential for growing your investment. This is why I always advocate to start investing as young as possible. I also encourage clients to teach their children effective investing practices at a young age. Think about it this way: If you hold Apple stock for one year, and receive a 2% dividend that is reinvested, you are not allowing the compounding effect to take place. If, on the other hand, you hold that same Apple stock for five or 10 years and reinvest dividends along the way, you give yourself a chance to harness the power of the compounding effect.

Unfortunately, there is one big downfall to compound interest: when you are not investing money, and borrow instead. This takes place with credit cards—when you charge something on your credit card, and do not pay it all the way off, you have a portion that is subject to interest. If you continue this pattern, the interest you pay may increase due to charging a larger balance. This is why it takes so long to pay off a credit card when you make the minimum payment.

Let's say you charge $10,000 on your credit card and pay a nine percent Annual Interest Rate (APR). You are also only paying $300 a month to pay off the debt. You will pay approximately $1,550.66 in interest, and it will take you roughly 39 months to pay off the debt. That is over 3 years of your life. This was a simple calculation, and your situation may be different based on how the interest is calculated. Some credit cards compound interest on a daily basis—but either way, this is a losing proposition. The scenario I outlined is based on not using that card again until the debt is paid off, but this is not realistic. Most people add debt to the balance even while paying it off, and this leads to a cycle of paying off credit cards and interest that is hard to break.

It is important to put compound interest on your side whenever you have a chance. If it is working against you through the form of credit cards and loans, it might make sense to focus on paying those off. At the same time focusing on beefing up your retirement should be a priority. Create a financial plan yourself, or work with a professional to help you navigate the rough terrain. Many consider compound interest a miracle, but it is fairly predictable and should be used to your advantage. Let compound interest build you up, and not tear you down.

Things to remember:

1) Reinvesting dividends and interest help investments grow faster.
2) The longer you can stay invested, the more powerful compound interest can affect your investments.
3) Compound interest is your enemy when it comes to debt.

Blueprint Your Investments

Lesson: An Investment Policy Statement is an important part of your investing toolkit and should not be neglected.

Building a portfolio without an Investment Policy Statement (IPS) is like building a home without a blueprint. When building a home, it is important to pre-plan the layout or floor plan, along with what materials will be used. An architect designs the plans to your specification. These plans can change during construction, but the general layout is likely maintained. Can you imagine what it would look like if you didn't have a blueprint? The bathroom could end up in the garage, or the bedroom could end up where you wanted the kitchen. Telling the builders what goes where would be chaos—you would make every decision spontaneously whether rational or not.

The same reasoning applies to your IPS. As mentioned in lesson one, a Financial Plan is the movie script for your life. Similarly, the IPS is the blueprint that builds the "set" for the movie to take place. It is a document that allows you to choose the type of investments or "materials" you would like. It lays out the allocation, or "floor plan." The document will also take into account any major life goals, such as purchasing a home or sending your children to school. You are essentially building what you would like your investment life to look like through a rational game plan. This plan increases your chances of achieving overall goals.

Below is a list of some components of a well-crafted IPS. This is not an exhaustive list, and the document is customizable—but this gets you started on what it takes to create your IPS.

Investment objectives and time horizon:
Include long-term and short-term goals, along with the amount of time you expect to be invested.

Risk/return profile:
Outline your expected return, and the amount of volatility and risk you are expecting to achieve that return.

Asset allocation and targets:
Create a current allocation of your investments to benchmark where your portfolio is now, and where you would like it to be in the future.

Rebalancing schedule: Set a reasonable expectation for how often your portfolio will be rebalanced to ensure risk and expected return will be reevaluated.

Liquidity requirements:
Dictate how liquid your investments need to be, along with cash flow needs.

Creating an IPS does take work. This is why, in spite of the importance of an IPS, many investors do not use them and don't know what one is—unless they previously hired or currently utilize a professional money manager. Out of the thousands of clients I have worked with that manage their own money, maybe five were working from an IPS before meeting me. A professional does not have a choice. When they have entered an advisory agreement, it is part of their duty to keep an IPS on file and review it regularly. An individual investor does not have a fiduciary responsibility to themselves. They often make investment decisions based on emotion, as opposed to the logic and reason that moves them towards objectives.

In 2008, one of the clearest examples of disaster striking for not having an IPS took place. This is not an isolated incident—I have seen this happen to many investors without an advisor or IPS. The market was doing well for quite some time before the crash. The overall stock market rose, which ballooned the equity allocation of many portfolios. Investors with moderate portfolios may have reallocated to aggressive portfolios because they never trimmed down the stock, which was growing quickly as a percentage of the portfolio. We know what happened next. Many saw their portfolio take on more losses than they would have if they had just rebalanced and stuck with a more moderate allocation. If you don't put your allocation in writing, it is virtually impossible to keep track of when to rebalance.

An investment policy statement has the ability to keep us focused when reviewed yearly. Many distractions come up in our investing lives—extreme upward or downward market swings can lead us off course. This causes us to become more aggressive or conservative than we need to be. I have conversations with clients about whether they are comfortable with the risk levels in their portfolios. I usually redirect the client's attention back to their goals and the reason why they are investing in the first place. This is because clients typically have a financial plan and an IPS in place. This gives us a blueprint to follow.

Creating an IPS does not have to be complicated. In most cases, having something is better than nothing. If you use an advisor, you likely already have one and review your plan regularly. If you are investing on your own, many tools and templates are available online. It is important to consider your Investment Policy Statement as a living document and have the ability to change it when necessary. An IPS will typically only change when major life events occur, such as having a child, getting married, or experiencing a liquidity event, like selling a business. You might also change the document to adjust risk levels depending on how your portfolio performs over an extended period of time.

When building your financial house, make sure you have a proper blueprint or IPS in place. It is well worth the planning. It means the difference between achieving your goals successfully, or falling short. It can also serve as a comfort tool to reference when a storm like 2008 strikes.

Things to remember:

1) An IPS is the blueprint for your investments.
2) Creating an IPS helps you stay focused on investment objectives.
3) Review your IPS regularly, and adjust it according to your situation.

REAL ESTATE REALITY CHECK

Lesson: Real estate can diversify your portfolio.

Owning rental properties may not be as glamorous as it looks. Watching television shows about riches to be had, and countless Facebook ads revealing "how to" get rich off real estate makes the allure attractive. Who wouldn't want to get paid for what some think is a "passive" business—but most things in life aren't always what they seem. Real estate is hard work. Whether you hire a property manager, or do it yourself, success takes attention and decision-making skills. Along the way, you will experience your own list of horror stories, which most professionals wear as badges of honor. A tenant once awakened me at 3 AM because their apartment flooded after the water heater broke overnight. Of course, this happened when he had family in town. I met his mother and father while we were all standing in puddles of water. Not a fun experience, but I wear this badge with pride.

Entering the real estate market takes more time and resources than most had initially planned. I once purchased a four-plex in Phoenix, Arizona, which was quite an experience. I was young and thought I'd focus on real estate. I lived in one of the apartments, and rented out the other three. It was great—I lived for free and if nothing went wrong that month, I pocketed a couple hundred dollars. I was very fortunate to have bought the property right after the 2008 crash, which gave me a very low price relative to the rent paid by tenants. It also gave me a lot of room for error, while still maintaining positive cash flow. I got lucky with that property. Today, in the same market as that property, margins have shrunk and there is little room for error if positive cash flow needs to be maintained. Most people do not get lucky like I did. They find real estate investing a little more complex than they initially imagined. However, this added complexity might prove to be a valuable part of your portfolio.

Clients often ask whether or not they should purchase physical real estate. Diversifying your overall portfolio with real estate can be beneficial. It may also provide you with current tax benefits. One factor in deciding to go down the real estate route is assessing whether or not you want to spend time on it. Real estate takes time. Many systems make a real estate portfolio less time consuming, but nonetheless something always comes up. Always! Decide how many hours a month you are willing to dedicate to this pursuit. How many additional phone calls you are willing to receive a month? How many more decisions are you willing to make? If you already talk to too many people a day in your profession, and do not have time for more phone calls, physical real estate might not be the best option for you.

Decipher whether real estate helps you diversify your investments or concentrate them. If the only asset you have after completing a real estate deal is that piece of property, then you now have a concentrated position, meaning your entire investment picture is painted by that one investment. This is not an ideal position. For some people, that has worked out nicely—if you purchased real estate 20+ years ago in Santa Monica, or many other parts of Southern California, that probably worked out well. If you purchased in an area where property values are stagnant, your values may not have risen at a rate that was high enough to concentrate your investment in that area. Since one of my major focuses with clients is diversifying assets, I am fond of adding real estate—but only when it makes sense, and does not completely concentrate net worth in that one sector.

There are financial pros to traversing real estate, but there are also cons. It can be expensive to secure finances, along with down payment money. Saving a sufficient down payment can put investment properties out of reach for many. Gaining exposure to real estate through the traditional route of Mutual Funds can be done with a much lower barrier to entry. Some mutual funds have low minimums. Of course, going the mutual fund route, you lose some potential tax benefits that may have been available through purchasing physical property—but it gets you invested quicker than saving up for a down payment.

Typically, your investment will not be very liquid. Some access equity by borrowing against the home with products like Home Equity Lines Of Credit (HELOC). But even these products do not let you tap into the full amount of equity that may be sitting in the property. A portion of your investment will always be illiquid, unless you sell. Selling in the wrong market because you need cash can be a quick way to turn a good real estate deal into a losing one.

Real estate could require unexpected additional investment. Things go wrong with properties. Just remember you will be cutting a check when anything goes wrong. You also pay legal fees for things that may unexpectedly rise due to owning a property. I understand different types of insurance will cover some things, but overall, you should expect to invest more than your down payment. Building a reserve is crucial. If that reserve is not built, and the emergency arises, you may find yourself scrambling to put together capital to fund an issue with your property.

To increase your odds of success in real estate, I encourage procuring a mentor. The mentor should have experience conducting the type of deals that you would like to do. You can save a lot of money, sweat equity and tears by finding a skilled mentor in the first place. One of my first mentor's multifamily apartment buildings was just like the one I purchased. Due to that mentor's guidance, I made fewer mistakes than I would have otherwise.

It is important to find and operate in a niche. Specialization in one or two markets is usually enough for most investors. Do you want to purchase single family homes, multifamily apartments or commercial real estate? Each one of these investments have completely different risk factors and market factors. The financing can also vary greatly. Because of the complexity, specializing can pay off big in the long run.

Many have lose and made a fortune off of the allure of real estate. Something about owning a physical property is attractive, and the idea of visiting your investment and touching it brings a sense of satisfaction. In the same respect, when everything goes wrong, you feel the pain of investing in a physical piece of property. You can't just hit a button and sell to make the pain dissipate—you have to work through every decision meticulously. Consider owning real estate as an investment closely, and if it isn't for you, don't give into the temptation. Just walk away.

Things to remember:

1) Ensure real estate complements your overall plan.
2) Find a mentor with experience in real estate.
3) Find your niche.

SIMPLIFY YOUR INVESTMENT LIFE

Lesson: Assess Risk, Time Horizon, and Diversification when making an investment decision.

For all that technology has brought into our investing lives, simplification isn't always one of the outcomes. I have trouble remembering passwords. Between all of the varying systems and accounts I hold, I probably have over 30 passwords. Many are ridiculously long, but length is important in maintaining security. I reset at least one password a week, and it no longer bothers me because I am not the only one in this situation. The more we try to simplify, the more we tend to complicate. That is why I find it understandable for an investor to want to simplify investment decisions. I am often asked to breakdown investment decisions in the most concise manner possible.

Making the investment decision process simple is no easy task. Just thinking about the different products that come out on a yearly basis is enough to drive someone crazy. As a professional, l I speak the financial "lingo" as a second tongue while evaluating products quickly and efficiently. If you are just starting out, or do not care to spend large amounts of time bringing yourself up to speed, this can be a daunting task. Even if you hire someone to do it for you, a general understanding of investments is necessary to feel at ease with your decisions. Otherwise, it's hard to decide whether or not an investment makes sense. Add the complication of different asset types and investment strategies, and you may be faced with a dilemma. To simplify investment decisions, I teach the following acronym: RTD.

R = Risk.
T = Time Horizon.
D = Diversification.

I should warn you that RTD is not a comprehensive approach. It serves as a guide in training your thought process to make informed investment decisions. Now, the three components of this acronym should not be treated independently. Think of them as three ingredients to make the perfect dish, and all must be present for you to commit capital to an investment. If the three ingredients do not work properly together, it might be time to walk away from the investment you are considering. At the least seek a second opinion, which may be more informed or qualified to provide guidance.

When considering the risk of an investment, your measuring device will vary. For an individual stock or stock portfolio, it may be easy to get that type of data by searching online. Work with a realtor to receive a proper evaluation on real estate. For any type of alternative investment, such as investing directly in a business, your risk level may be more subjective. The goal is to have an informed opinion on the past risk of the investment, and understand that future risk levels could be different. The benefit of knowing this information should be obvious. You are essentially gauging how much you are willing to lose on the investment if you are wrong. Are you willing to lose 10%, 50% or even all of your investment? Knowing this information is crucial to your success as an investor.

Consider how long you have to hold the investment. If you are in a very aggressive managed stock portfolio, your advisor may tell you it is preferable to hold the portfolio for 10 or more years. Make sure that you are comfortable with that before making the investment. If you were thinking of only keeping the money in the market for one or two years, it might not make sense to be aggressive in the stock market—especially if you need capital for something important, like a down payment on a home. When you purchase a home, ask yourself how long you plan on keeping it. Is this a home you're going to purchase and sell within one or two years, or is this home where you plan on raising your family? Ask yourself these questions when deciding to make the investment.

Finally, after you have assessed the risk and the time horizon, take a deep look at whether or not the new investment fits into your current portfolio. Will adding this new investment give you a really concentrated position, or will it complement the diversification model you have been using? This is fundamental to my outlook on investing. Diversification is always a factor, and diversifying your portfolio is subjective. You should ultimately work that out with a professional on a one on one basis. Once you have an answer on diversification, you will be able to better decide if further research makes sense, or if it's time to walk away.

Just like it is not safe to have one password for every account you hold, the RTD acronym is not meant to be a one-size-fits-all solution. It's meant to help you efficiently sift through opportunities and allows you to make more informed decisions faster. Sometimes, simplification is the best route to provide clarity on pursuing an investment option.

Things to remember:

1) Evaluate the risk of an investment before committing capital.
2) Consider the necessary holding period to achieve your desired return.
3) Assess whether a new investment fits into your current portfolio.

SIZE DOESN'T MATTER

Lesson: Small businesses can benefit from established retirement plans.

If you ask a business owner what their best investment is, many will claim it is their business itself. This is understandable because a business is like your child. You give birth to an idea. You care for it, watch it grow and are there for the good times and bad. Nurturing your business can rightfully or wrongfully become the center of your life. At times, the emotional attachment to your business may not allow you to see the bigger picture. Just like a parent might be blinded to inadequacies of their children, the same goes for a business. However, more is going on in the investment world than what is taking place in your business alone.

After working with thousands of business owners, I find that many neglect a basic business retirement plan—this is an extremely costly mistake. The reasons for non-participation in retirement plans vary from business owner to business owner. Some believe their business is too small for a retirement plan. Clients have said, "It's just me Adam. I don't need a retirement plan for my employees, because I am the only employee." But this is not a real reason. Retirement plans exist that benefit one-person shops.

Others believe that the cost of maintaining a plan is out of reach. The thought of having an administrator, and one more meeting a year to discuss financial matters, makes most business owners cringe—especially when they are knee deep in running their current business. This is also incorrect. Retirement plans exist that require little to no additional paperwork and maintenance.

Some have not explored the value of potential tax benefits associated with retirement plans. Not knowing the financial benefits leads to leaving tax benefits unexplored. You should not assume that your CPA is also versed in retirement plans because this is not always the case. Just because someone files your taxes does not mean they are qualified to provide advice on business retirement planning. Remember, your CPA is mostly focused on write offs and compliance. They are not keeping abreast the latest developments in retirement planning for business owners. I receive referrals from CPAs that seek my expertise in retirement planning for their client. The best case scenario is a CPA that works closely with your financial advisor in this situation.

I recommend that business owners do an analysis of their current situation to see if a retirement plan makes sense. In establishing a retirement plan that has little to no cost, many small businesses benefit immediately. Below is a list of just a few retirement plan options for small business owners. This is not an exhaustive list, but starts you on your search.

<u>Common Small Business Retirement Plans:</u>
Simplified Employee Pension - SEP IRA - A plan where the employer makes contributions instead of the employee;

SIMPLE IRA - A plan where the employee makes the majority of the contributions, wile the employer makes a small match;

Individual 401(k) - A plan for businesses that do not have employees defined by regulation, and would like to make profit sharing and deferral contributions to maximize contributions;

I encourage you to further research the above plans to learn their nuances. The information I provided is meant to whet your appetite for more. My goal is to spark your interest and find something that works for your specific situation.

Employee retention is often not considered by business owners when setting up a retirement plan is. I am not one to rely on statistics about employment from studies, because numbers can be made to read just about anything. In this case, however, everything I have read throughout the years has pointed to retirement plans benefiting most industries and improving employee retention. This may or may not be true for your field, business or industry. If the company shows they care by giving retirement benefits to employees, the employee is likely to stick around a little longer than if they were receiving additional benefits. How much a company spends to keep an employee around is decided on a case-by-case basis, but if the cost is relatively low, it makes sense to spend the money on offering a retirement plan.

Business owners should also consider the idea of diversifying investments to spread the risk across various instruments. When a business owner reinvests all his capital into their business, they create an extremely concentrated position. Their future financial picture may completely ride on the success or failure of their business. When you invest in a retirement plan, you diversify your financial holdings. You now have assets invested in other companies, which may be spread throughout the world. This is done through purchasing stock and other equity investments. Do not neglect this concept. If your business fails, or something unexpected occurs that leads to you not being able to sell your business, you will at least have retirement plan assets.

I understand that in a business owner's eyes, your business will probably always be priority where you invest your money. Just like a mother may think her child can do no wrong, you will look at your business in a similar way. It can do no wrong regardless of its current or future state—I only ask that you consider a larger investment world and diversifying it.

Things to remember:

1) Establish a retirement plan for your business as soon as it is feasible, regardless of its size.
2) Tax and other benefits may be available.
3) Contributing to your retirement plan diversifies your investment life.

PART 3

FAMILY FINANCIAL SUCCESS

FAMILY FEUDS CAN HAPPEN TO ANYONE

Lesson: Estate Plans keep your family together after you are gone.

D o you really know what will happen when you pass on? I'm not referring to afterlife, or whatever you believe in. I'm asking what will happen to your family and loved ones—the people you care about most? You may leave enough of a legacy to take care of them, but sometimes money, is not enough. They need an estate plan. An estate plan is a blueprint for how you would like assets and other important items dealt with in the case of death or incapacitation. If you die or become incapacitate, not having an estate plan can put your family in a terrible situation.

Lack of an estate plan can destroy your family's harmony for decades, or even permanently. I find that this happens quite often, especially when the first grandparents or parents with the majority of the wealth pass on. Siblings who were the best of friends have stopped talking. Marriages have ended due to the stress of a brutal court battle over inherited assets. Children stop talking to parents because they felt unfairly treated in their grandparents' will. You may be thinking this could never happen to you and your family, however, I am telling you from experience that it most definitely could.

People change when somebody passes, and I do not know all the reasons why. Maybe the sense of loss causes us to act in ways we could not imagine, and the feeling of helplessness when a loved one is no longer around. Maybe the internal greed mechanism that is hardwired in our brains ignite after inheriting money we did not earn. I don't really know why people act the way they do in these situations, but what I do know is the problem can be taken care of ahead of time without incurring too much cost.

Estate plans vary in complexity, depending on your situation. They may include a will and medical directives. The cost ranges widely from a couple hundred to thousands of dollars, but the cost can be outweighed by the peace of mind from knowing your last wishes will be carried out correctly. In addition, decreasing the risk of family feuds is priceless.

Below is a list of some of the items that can be included in an estate plan:

Health care power of attorney:
Allows another individual to make important health care decisions for you if you become incapacitated.

Guardianship designations:
Allows you to designate who takes care of your child if both parents pass. If this is not in place, the courts decide what may be in your child's best interest.

Will/Trust:
Ensures property is passed on according to your wishes. Without a will/trust, the distribution of your assets can be a costly and emotional mess for your heirs.

Durable power of attorney:
Allows you to designate who makes financial decisions for you if you become incapacitated. If you do not choose this person, the courts will.

Letter of intent:
A document you leave to your executor or beneficiary. It tells them what you want done after your death or incapacitation. It also allows you to make special requests.

Beneficiary designations:
Allows you to pass along assets in an efficient manner, without necessarily going through the courts. This may include 401(k) s and IRAs.

The above is a simplified list with many different implications. It is important to work with an estate attorney and financial advisor on these items. The estate attorney draws up the legal documents, and the financial advisor works with the attorney to bring the overall plan together. It is also important to review these documents. If you created a trust 10 or 20 years ago, and have not had an attorney review it, you might be missing important items. Laws and rules change. Your estate plan is a living document that changes along with laws and your personal situation. You cannot create and forget estate plans; they do not care for themselves.

Most people do not want to talk about what happens to their money when they pass on. Discussing mortality is an uncomfortable subject because it reminds us that we cannot live forever. If you are not convinced to complete an estate plan, I'll leave you with one last bit of advice. It is far less costly to deal with it now than later. Entire multi-million-dollar estates have nearly vanished from legal fees of feuding families. A person does not work their entire life to build an estate just to pay court costs and lawyers. They intended those assets to be part of their legacy, and to help their family. What do you intend your legacy to be?

Things to remember:

1) Discussing mortality is uncomfortable, but we must do it anyway.
2) Estate plans increase the chance of your family still getting along after you pass.
3) Legal fees for creating an estate plan are typically much less than the fees of not having one in place—especially if settling the estate goes to court.

ARE YOUR CHILDREN FINANCIAL ILLITERATES?

Lesson: Teaching children money at a young age gives them an advantage in life.

I t is safe to say that most parents want their children to be literate. Giving your child the gift of reading is a basic necessity in most United States households. Not many parents say, "I don't want my child to be able to read." However, most parents completely neglect providing their children with something that is just as important: financial education. The reason for this varies.

Some parents believe their children will learn money concepts at some point in school, but this may or may not happen. Other parents might be in the dark when regarding their own finances, and do not attempt to teach what they do not know themselves. In some cultures, talking about money is an embarrassing topic that should not be brought up. While these may all seem like valid reasons, and some of you may fit into these categories, you must break the cycle if you want your children to have a chance at getting ahead.

As a kid, I do not recall my parents teaching me about money, other than to make it and save as much as possible. This education might not have been the best, but it was something. My parents fall into the category of parents not understanding finances, so they chose to not attempt teaching it. They did know the basics, like balancing a bank account and basic debt topics. But investing in the markets or planning for retirement and financial security were not topics I recall ever being brought up. In fact, it wasn't until I was an adult that I brought these topics to the forefront.

What my parents did do was leverage the talents of others. My parents brought financially savvy people into my life that understood money concepts more than they did. These mentors included business owners with a better-rounded education on money. Seek out mentors and other education resources that your children can absorb. The amount of available free information makes it possible for everyone to receive a financial education. Watch a YouTube video about money with the family, and discuss new learnings afterwards. Small steps add up over time.

You can educate yourself and your family at the same time. I coach my clients to have meetings with their children about the family's finances. Don't necessarily disclose bank balances, but talk about items that matter to the children and the parents alike. For example, if your child is really young, you might include him or her in planning the family vacation. How much is Disneyland going to cost? How much for the hotel? What is the budget for food? After the vacation is over, have another meeting and decipher whether or not the family stayed within the "budget." If the child is a little older, it makes sense to discuss what type of account money should be held in. Have them look up bank interest rates online. Interest rates may be low now, but that is not the point. Just involve them in the exercise—trust me, these habits will stick and serve your children down the line.

Meetings will vary from household to household, but they are effective in getting your child comfortable with talking about money to grownups and other authority figures. This is extremely important. Many times, a person's first time talking with professional about finances is when they stumble into a firm a couple years out of college because they have a question about investing. Some people do not meet with an advisor until much later. In fact, some clients bring their children to meetings with me once or twice a year. I have had 12-year-olds in meetings that were extremely savvy and well spoken in finance, because their parents did some of the things I advise you to do.

If your child is older, consider having him read a book on money for their age group. Have them present what they learned to the family, and tie this assignment to some type of reward. When I was young, my parents allowed me to earn an allowance by writing book reports. I remember picking out a book at the library with my dad to earn that week's allowance. Taking out the trash and helping out around the house was required—writing a book report was an extra and rewarded with allowance.

Make learning about money and finances fun for your children. Get creative! All too many times, I meet with a person making a six-figure salary, and they have no clue how money works. If this is you, you have time to correct this—just start now. My goal is to prevent clients' children from falling into this category. It should be your goal that none of your children fall into this category either.

Things to remember:

1) Teach your children money concepts early in life, and continue this education throughout their lives.
2) If you are not comfortable with educating your child on money, outsource the task to mentors, videos and books.
3) Get creative and keep your child engaged.

ARM YOUR KIDS FOR SUCCESS

Lesson: Program your kids with investment habits early.

Not picking that lucky stock is not the biggest regret of my investing career. Picking a winner does feel great. If you bought Amazon in a large enough amount when it was first listed on the stock market, you may have been set for life—but we cannot always control that scenario. I was 100% in control of my biggest regret. My biggest regret is that I did not start investing sooner. I mean much sooner.

I remember being lectured from one of my early mentors in the financial services business. "Adam, you have earned income this year. You should start contributing to a Roth IRA." I received these words of wisdom when I was 16. To make matters worse, I was actually working for a brokerage firm. It's not like it would have been a large expenditure of energy—but I didn't listen. I didn't understand the importance of putting $100.00 a paycheck into a retirement account. I hope you do after reading about compound interest. If you do not remember what I am talking about, go back and review.

I didn't open my first retirement account until sometime later. Part of the reason for not investing earlier was that I was raised in a saving culture, and not an investing culture. Many households teach their children to save, but do not transition them into investing. This is a big mistake that can have a lasting impression on your child's life. While I had already accumulated quite a few assets for somebody my age, I hadn't transitioned into the investor mindset. The effect of this was losing many years of tax benefited investing and wasted money.

I was apt to spend savings on frivolous things. I remember pouring money into an old Camaro—I loved cars so I invested in fixing it up and had fun. I thought one day, I may sell it for a profit. That was silly of me. If I had taken that same money and invested it, at this point in my life—even at a modest return of $5,000—it could have easily tripled. By the time I hit retirement, it could have been over $50,000 of tax-free money if I had invested in a Roth account. While $50,000 won't make or break my retirement, those investing habits would have carried over into my life sooner. I would have assuredly made more contributions as I saw my investments rise over the years. Programing the habit is key. Instead, I didn't, and I can barely even remember many of the luxury items I wasted money on throughout the years. As for the Camaro—because I know you are wondering—it is somewhere in the junkyard.

I encourage anyone with children to start their investing at a young age. There are many types of accounts that can be opened in a child's name inexpensively, and controlled by the parent. I am not saying that you must open a retirement account for your child, but transitioning from teaching savings to investing would be beneficial.

Below is a list of some accounts available for minors that a parent can control:

Custodial account/ Uniform Transfers To Minors Act (UTMA)/ Uniform Gifts To Minors Act (UGMA):
This brokerage account offers the parent complete control, and can be signed over when the child is no longer a minor.

529 Plan:
A college savings plan for higher education.

Educational Savings Account (ESA):
This plan allows you to save for education with more flexibility than a 529 Plan.

The above outlined accounts are great options for teaching children about saving and investing. Each account has very specific rules, tax consequences and regulations. Consult your advisor to determine which, if any, work for your situation.

You may have previously taken your child to the bank to open an account. I remember opening my first bank account with my father. It was a thing of pride. Do not stop doing that, but try adding some type of investment account to the mix. I encourage clients with children to bring them into my office so we can speak start them off young. You would be surprised to find how much children can learn about investing and how fast they pick up the concepts—sometimes faster than their parents! The amount invested doesn't have to be substantial. There are many mutual funds out there that have extremely low minimums, some well under $100. Once this account is open, however, you might give the child the decision of whether they want to receive a video game for their next birthday or a contribution to their investment account. It may surprise you to find they opt for the investment account contribution.

If you want your kids to have the best possible chance at a successful investing life, start them out young. You wouldn't want them to look back on their lives and wonder why they hadn't started investing sooner—good investing habits last a lifetime.

Things to remember:

1) Transition from teaching your kids solely the savings habit. Instead, include the investing habit also.
2) Many options for investing exist that have low dollar commitment amounts.
3) Give your kids the opportunity to make contributions to their accounts, instead of receiving toys and other non-assets.

EDUCATION COSTS CAN KILL YOUR RETIREMENT

Lesson: Don't neglect saving for retirement while funding your children's education.

Sending your children to college shouldn't be a crisis that demands all resources. It has become increasingly difficult to receive employment without a college degree, and the workforce is now competing for jobs worldwide. It has almost become a bare minimum to have some type of college education, and it isn't getting any cheaper. You could buy a Ferrari for the cost of sending your children to college today, and this trend is likely to continue for the rest of our lives.

There are ways to get ahead of the huge financial commitment that college entails. Start saving for your children's education as soon as possible. I recommend opening up some type of account that is earmarked for education when children are born. If you need a refresher on why it is important to start young, reflect back on the chapter "Experience Compound Interest." This is a vital part of your financial plan. For some clients, opening a 529 plan is a simple solution to saving for their children's education. This plan has various potential tax benefits. These benefits can make it more cost effective for you to pay for a portion—or all—of your children's college. To find out whether or not a 529 plan works for you, consult with your tax consultant or financial advisor.

An interesting paradox usually exists when a child is young and the parents immediately need to begin saving for retirement. It's extremely obvious when you consider the factors. When someone is younger and starting a family, they are typically in leaner earning years than they will be further down the line. This is because they are usually in junior positions in their careers. This is also one of the most important times for them to begin saving for retirement. At the same time, saving for their children's education is a must if a parent wants to absorb these costs. So the parent is faced with a dilemma. Even if it is a balancing act, what goal should take priority?

One thing I always communicate to clients is that children will likely be able to take out loans for college, but you cannot take out a loan for retirement. This is a really important concept to keep in mind because many households have fallen short in funding retirement due to spending too much on their children's education. The parent might believe they are being responsible in satisfying the urge to help their children out, but this is not always the case. It is pretty commonplace for a college graduate to not be fully self-sufficient after graduating college. Typically, parents will subsidize their children's lifestyle for many years after college. How many of you still pay for your college graduate's rent and car payment? And what if they decide they want an advanced degree? I have seen a trend of college graduates going back for further education just because they cannot find a job, or the college atmosphere is preferable to actually working.

What has changed in the system that makes it more preferable to fund your retirement than a child's education? In the past, it was commonplace for a child to take care of their parents as they aged. In fact, it was pretty much assumed that this would take place. At that point in time, retirement was your children, a pension and maybe social security. This model has changed and is why it is so important to place retirement at an equal—if not higher—level of importance as your child's education. Pensions are virtually nonexistent and many consider social security questionable. Investing in your child's education isn't even what is used to be.

The fact of the matter is that spending money on education does not guarantee a child's success or a high enough compensation to ensure they will be financially able to care for you in the future. Many times, a parent ends up moving back in with their children later down the line because they do not have sufficient savings to pay for a proper retirement home. This puts a lot of stress on the household they enter, especially when caregivers come in and out. The living situation can get uncomfortable and becomes extremely stressful on marriages.

For the record, I love my parents and would welcome them anytime. I hope you do not think this lesson is too harsh. I am laying out the realities that are rarely talked about when it comes to funding retirement and education tradeoff. The scenarios play out in both good ways and bad. You ultimately have to decide what works best for you. Education doesn't have to be a scary proposition. Start planning young and keep the big picture in mind at all times, and you will have choices in the future of what route makes the most sense for you.

Things to remember:

1) Kids can borrow for education, but you can't borrow for retirement.
2) You may be able to use tax-benefited options for saving.
3) A college education isn't getting any cheaper. Start saving now.

GET AHEAD OF DIVORCE

Lesson: Both spouses should be involved in financial decision-making.

Many families segregate responsibilities. One spouse deals with finances, while the other takes care of maintenances around the home. Taking care of children is usually a joint endeavor, although one parent might take lead on certain items. Roles are usually doled out to kids, including chores and pitching in on areas that are needed. This makes sense to me. You want to run a household as efficiently as possible, and not duplicate responsibilities. One responsibility that should be a joint endeavor—but usually is not—is reviewing family finances. Communication about family finances should rank towards the top of the list for spouses to discuss.

Money issues are one of the top reasons for divorce in the United States today. This is understandable, considering the importance money plays in our day-to-day lives. This lack of communication typically comes from one spouse being disinterested in the subject or overbearing regarding finances. When I ask them to take a more active role in financial decisions, I receive quite a bit of pushback from the uninterested spouse. I also receive responses like "I'm too busy," "that's not my job," or "He or she takes care of that." I understand the hesitation, because it's not fun to learn a skill that you may not be accustomed to or care about. But in realizing that finances are at the root of many divorces, it makes sense to open these communication lines.

Both spouses must be aware of where the family stands financially to make sound financial decisions. As an outsider looking in, a disconnect occurs when finances are not reviewed by both spouses because one spouse thinks the family's financials stand in a completely different place than where they actually are. For example, it's not uncommon to hear one spouse bring up their desire to purchase a new car, while the other spouse brings up the fact that they are currently behind in bills. When I see these things happen, it is extremely obvious to me that these issues may lead to bigger ones down the line. So how do you stay ahead of this?

I recommend that spouses hold at least quarterly meetings. Monthly meetings are preferable because bills are usually paid once a month. Some families hold weekly meetings to discuss family finances. In these meetings, cover your current income and expenses. Review any investments you have and updated performance. This should all be done in writing. You don't have to do anything fancy, but you should put everything into a word document, Excel document or even handwritten on a pad of paper. It needs to be written down is because it becomes more real once it is. Having meetings also allows you to plan ahead for larger expenses that may happen down the line.

The last reason why spouses need to communicate is a sensitive subject. In my career, I have unfortunately seen this scenario play out many times. It is when a spouse passes away unexpectedly. When the surviving spouse has not dealt with the family's finances, and the burden is suddenly on their shoulders, it can really compound the pain of loss. It is just one more thing they have to deal with. Many times, they make poor decisions that alter their entire financial future because they are not accustomed to making financial decisions. This includes buying large items that are not in the budget, or even emotional spending. Paying bills seems like moving a mountain if you do not know whether the homeowner association dues are paid automatically or by a written check being written. Multiply this issue by twenty different bills that need to be paid, and you can see how these issues pile up quickly.

Money is one of the most intimate subjects. Our financial status makes up a part of our identity and the way we are perceived by society. Healthy discussion around finance is vital to keeping the family healthy and together down the line, so start monthly family meetings that will lead to a happier life.

Things to remember:

1) Finances are the root of many divorces.
2) Both spouses must understand where the family stands financially.
3) Hold regular family meetings to discuss finances in depth.

CONCLUSION

As humans, we all have some of the same basic needs. In my opinion, one of these needs is to feel unique and special. I am all for this concept. Our individuality and ability to express ourselves is one of the things that brings richness to our world. However, this craving to be unique does not necessarily benefit us when we apply it to our financial situation. Most of us can benefit from guidelines that have helped many others.

This book is meant to serve as a guide for you on your financial journey. Many of you may have found ideas you liked and some you dismissed. This is common when reading stories about the experiences of others, but I encourage you to revisit the concepts that caused discomfort and ask yourself: "How can I make this work in my life?" Instead of saying: "This doesn't apply to me because (fill in the blank here)." For example, maybe you were set on buying a home when it may not make sense for you. Do more research to see if buying a home is an emotional decision for you, or if it makes financial sense.

The brain is lazy, so it will tend to gravitate to what is comfortable. This includes concepts you already knew or were using. The other concepts will have to be massaged gently into your brain. If you didn't understand something, research it further to gain a better understanding of my position. For example, do robo-advisors make sense for you? Well you have heard my argument, now it is time for you to assess your situation.

Each and every chapter of this book was crafted from my experience in working with thousands of clients. The advice is practical. I have these types of conversations daily with clients and potential new clients.

Some of the most important takeaways are:

1) Create a financial plan.
2) Create an investment policy statement.
3) Diversify investments.
4) Create an emergency fund.

How many of you have completed all of the points mentioned above? If you haven't, start now. This is a financial journey. Your goals may not be reached in a day, but for many of you, reaching them is possible.

I hope that you are now convinced to take charge of your financial future. Quick actions, such as automatic investment, can ultimately lead to a habit that carries you through the rest of your life comfortably. But you must take action. Your actions now may affect how the rest of your life is lived.

APPENDIX

I look forward to walking with you on your journey to financial independence. I welcome you into my family.

Connect with Adam:

YouTube: Ask Adam Torres

Facebook: Ask Adam Torres

Webpage: AskAdamTorres.com

Periscope: @askadamtorres

SC | @askadamtorres

Twitter: @askadamtorres

Instagram: Ask Adam Torres

Connect with Century City Wealth Management, LLC:

Webpage: CenturyCityWealthManagement.com

About the Author

Adam Torres wrote *Money Matters* because he wanted to give readers a personal-finance manual written by someone qualified to help them succeed.

Torres is more than qualified. He is the CEO of Century City Wealth Management, LLC, a firm that helps families, organizations, and foundations make wise investment decisions.

Torres has spent more than eleven years consulting and advising more than a thousand business owners and three thousand families. He specializes in high-net-worth financial planning and has advised families with a cumulative net worth of more than $500 million.

In addition to financial planning, Torres gives speeches internationally on wealth management, leadership, team building, and change. He also founded Mr. Century City, LLC, a media, entertainment, and technology company with global reach.